KARATE for KIDS

J. ALLEN QUEEN

Sterling Publishing Co., Inc. New York

To my son, Alex

Photography by Samuel Jones, III
Edited by Claire Bazinet

Library of Congress Cataloging-in-Publication Data

Queen, J. Allen.
Karate for kids / J. Allen Queen.
p. cm.
Includes index.
ISBN 0-8069-0614-6
1. Karate for children—Juvenile literature. [1. Karate.]
I. Title.
GV1114.32.Q435 1994 93-45837
796.8′153—dc20 CIP
AC

10 9 8 7 6 5 4 3 2 1

Published by Sterling Publishing Company, Inc.
387 Park Avenue South, New York, N.Y. 10016

Distributed in Canada by Sterling Publishing
℅ Canadian Manda Group, P.O. Box 920, Station U
Toronto, Ontario, Canada M8Z 5P9
Distributed in Great Britain and Europe by Cassell PLC
Villiers House, 41/47 Strand, London WC2N 5JE, England
Distributed in Australia by Capricorn Link (Australia) Pty Ltd.
P.O. Box 6651, Baulkham Hills, Business Centre, NSW 2153, Australia
Manufactured in the United States of America

Sterling ISBN 0-8069-0614-6

Contents

The World of Karate

Hello, my name is Dr. Queen. I am a karate teacher and I am going to teach you how to do karate.

You can enjoy doing karate in a group or by yourself.

If you follow my directions, you will learn fast.

Before long you will be doing kicks like these karate students.

You will have fun learning karate.

First, you will learn how to do warm-up exercises, . . .

. . . then learn to do the karate punch, . . .

. . . and how to do kicks.

In this book, you will learn how to block, . . .

. . . do the karate chop, . . .

. . . and spar with an opponent.

You will also learn how to do the "karate dance," . . .

. . . and how to use your body for self-defense.

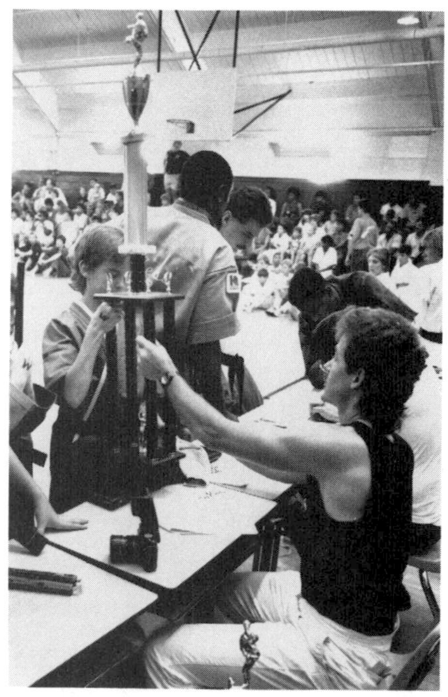

As in other sports, you can win trophies and awards.

At tournaments you can try out your karate skills . . .

. . . sparring with opponents who are your size and age.

In karate, you show respect to your instructor and your opponents by bowing.

You will learn discipline and how to work hard to earn a black belt. When you get the black belt, you will be a karate expert. The black belt is the highest honor in karate.

Are you like these boys and girls who are ready to learn karate?

If you are, follow me and let me get you started in the exciting world of karate.

Getting Started

To do karate, you need to wear loose clothing, such as a sweatsuit or a karate suit, called a gi (pronounced *gee*). You can order a gi from places that advertise in karate magazines.

Meditate

To be a true karate student, you must learn how to meditate, or clear your mind, for karate practice.

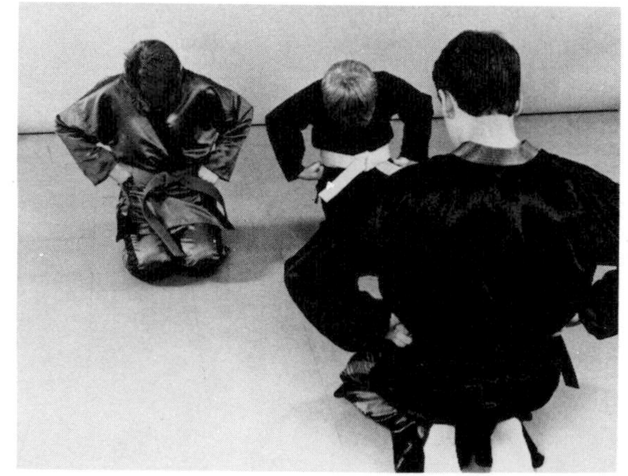

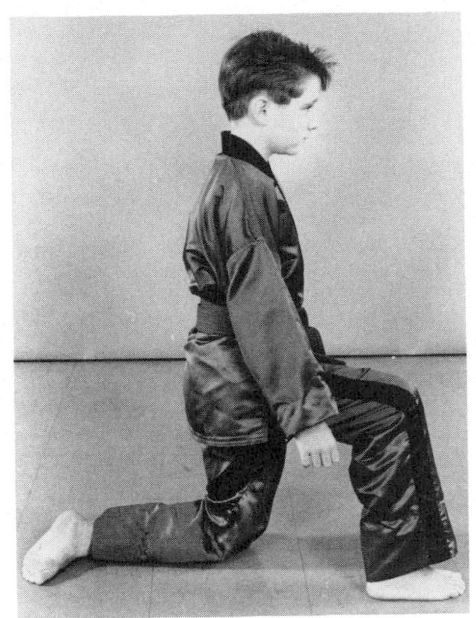

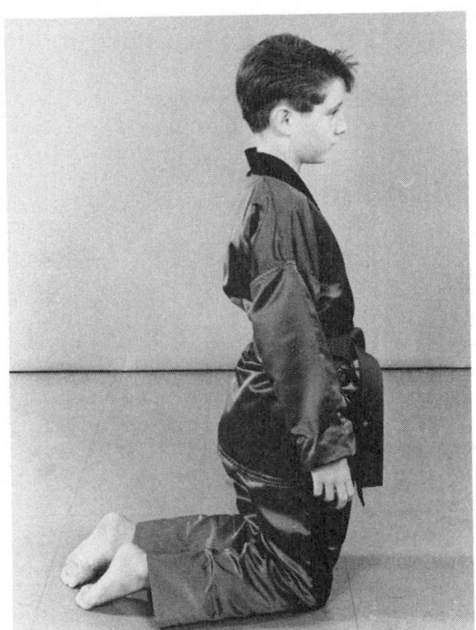

To meditate, first place your left knee on the floor . . . and then your right knee.

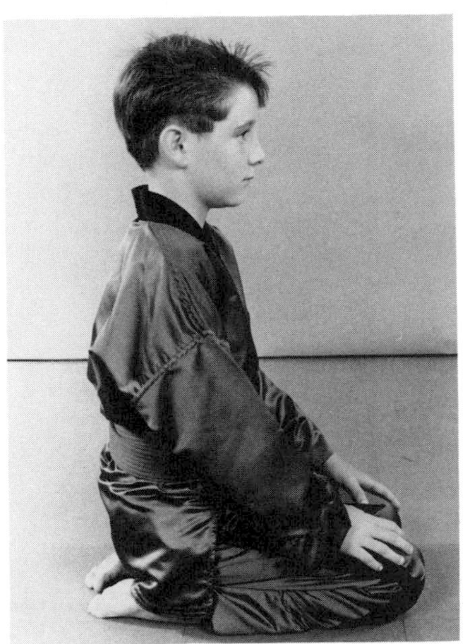

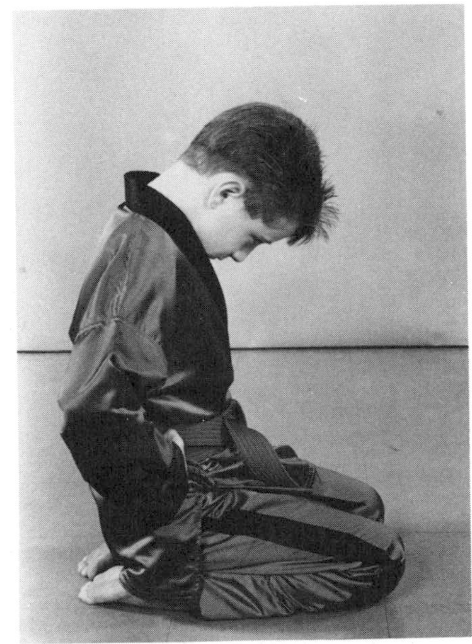

Sit back on your heels and . . . lower your head, placing your hands at your sides. Just think about what you are getting ready to do, which is to practise karate. Try not to think of anything else.

After a minute or so of meditation, get up and bow.

Bowing

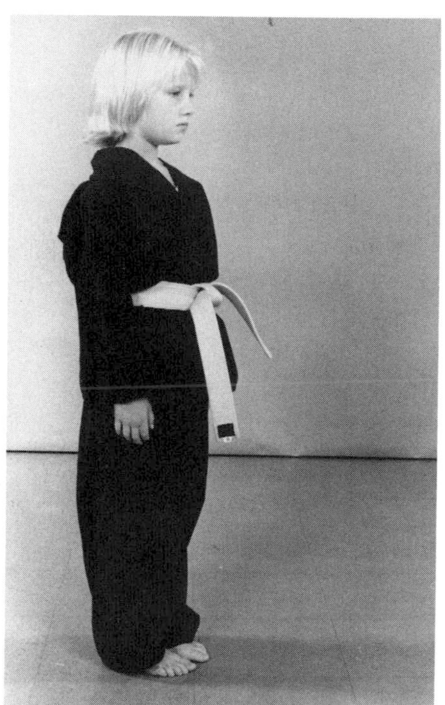

To bow, stand up straight with your feet together and your hands by your sides.

Shift your upper-body forward, while keeping your legs straight.

You will always begin and end your karate practice with the bow. This is the way you show respect.

You also bow to the karate instructor . . .

. . . and bow when you begin and end a sparring match. Showing respect is very important in karate.

You are now ready to warm up for karate. You will do exercises to get your body ready for practice.

Warm-Up Exercises

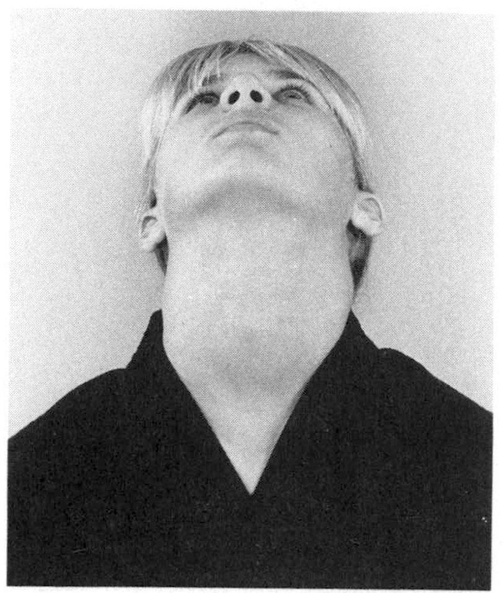

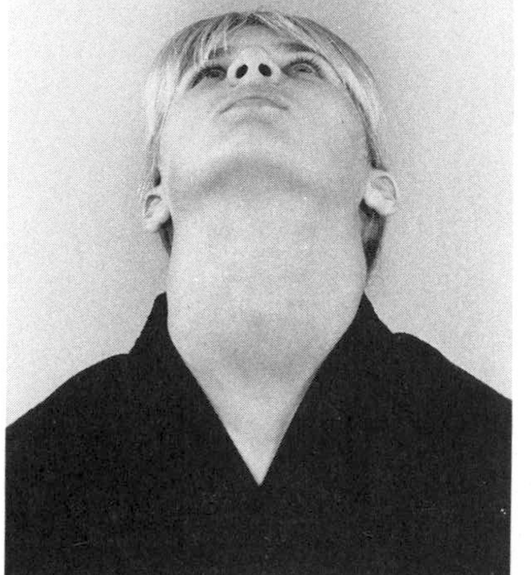

For the first exercise, pull your head back and stretch your neck.

Continue the exercise by moving your head to your right, . . .

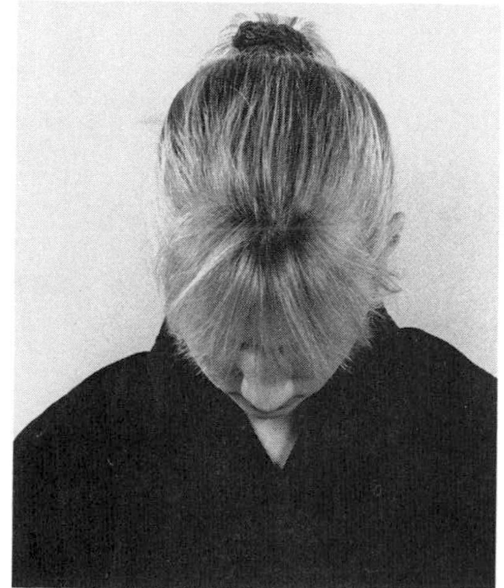

. . . and then to the front.

Finish by moving your head to the left.

Repeat this neck exercise slowly five times, from beginning to end.

To warm up the arms and upper body, make a circle. First, hold your right arm up in the air.

Stretch your arm out behind you.

Bring your arm down and around . . .

. . . until your arm is in front of you. Make the circle slowly five times with your left arm, then do the arm circle with the right arm.

Now make circles with both arms together. Start by bringing both arms straight up in the air, . . .

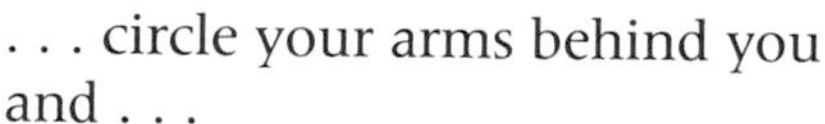

. . . circle your arms behind you and . . .

. . . then slowly continue the circle down, ending by stretching your hands out in front of you. Slowly, make the two-arm circle five times.

Next, stand with your arms straight out at your sides, like a plane.

Keep your arms straight out and swing your body to your left as far as possible.

When you have turned as far as possible without it hurting, swing your body around to your right as far as you can. Repeat the swings to the left and then to the right five times.

Important! Exercise should *not* hurt. Never push yourself to the point where you feel pain. If you get hurt doing exercises, you will not be able to practise karate.

Now you need to start warming up the lower body as you continue stretching your upper-body muscles. Stand with your feet wide apart and your hands touching up over your head. Do not bend your knees and do not bounce up and down. Do this and all exercises slowly.

Bend down and try to touch the floor with the tips of your fingers or the palms of your hands. Try not to bend your knees. Do this exercise five times.

Continuing this exercise, bring your legs closer together. Remember to start by putting your arms straight above your head.

Bend down and try to touch the floor. Go only as far as you can. Remember, do not bounce, and stop right away if it begins to hurt. Do this exercise five times.

After you can do the floor-touch exercise easily with your feet slightly apart, stand and place your feet *together*, and then bend forward and try to touch the floor. Be careful not to hurt yourself.

You are now ready to stretch your leg muscles a little more. Sit down with your right leg behind you and your left leg straight out in front of you.

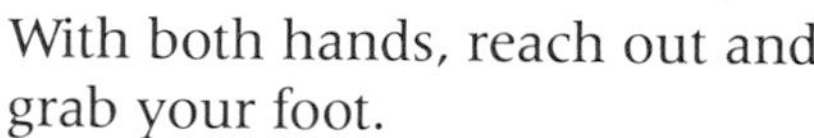

With both hands, reach out and grab your foot.

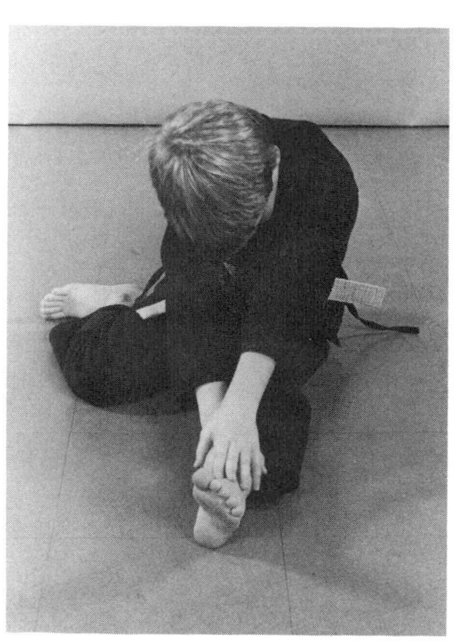

Next, bend your body forward and stretch out. Try to put your head down to your knee as you reach for your feet. Do this stretching exercise five times. Then place your left leg behind you and put your right leg out. Repeat the exercise, now with the opposite legs, five times in the same way as you did before.

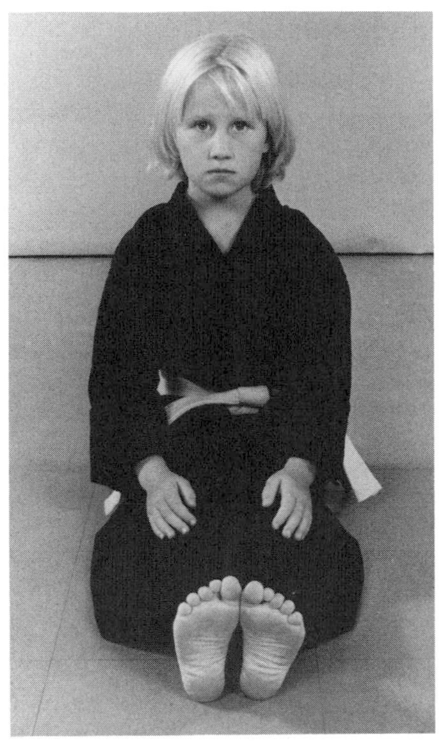

Sit down and place both of your legs out in front of you.

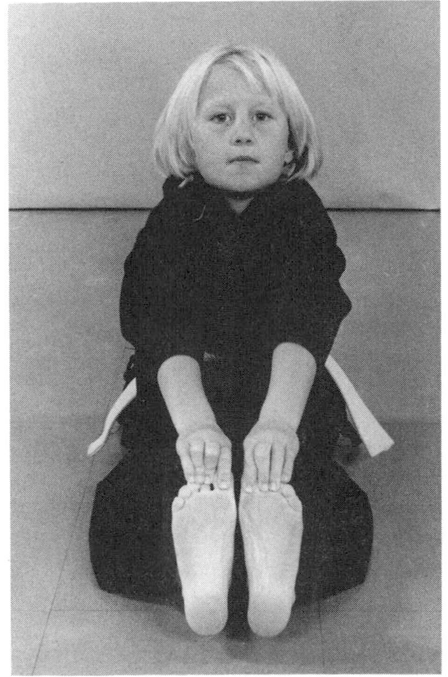

Reach out and grab your toes and lift up both of your feet. Hold up your feet as you count slowly to three. Repeat this exercise five times.

For this last exercise, it is important to go *very* slowly. Go only as far as you can stretch without any pain. To start, turn your head and left foot to your left.

Keep your right leg straight and push it out behind you as you begin to lower your body into a split.

Lower your body as far down as you can by pushing your right leg far behind you and your left leg forward in front of you. Place your hands on the floor to help you keep your balance. Do this left split one time and then get up, face to your right, and do a right split.

Remember to be very careful. You will get better results by going slowly. You can hurt yourself if you do these exercises too fast or too hard. Take your time, be careful, and you will be happy with your progress.

You are now ready to learn how to make a fist and do a karate punch. You will learn this, and the basic stances, blocks, strikes, and kicks in the next chapter.

Karate Basics

The karate punch is one of the major strikes in karate.

The Fist

To learn to make a fist for a karate punch: Put both of your arms up in the air with your hands open **(1)**.

Fold your fingertips in tightly towards your hands **(2)**.

Then roll your fingers and hands into fists **(3)**.

1

2

3

The Punch

Bring your hands down, . . .

. . . put your fists together, and . . .

. . . pull your left hand back so that it is upside down by your left side. Leave your right hand straight out.

To punch, begin to pull your right hand back as you push the left hand out.

Push into a punch. You can see that the right hand is now resting by your right side in an upside down position.

Turn the left hand for a punch, as you continue to pull the right arm back.

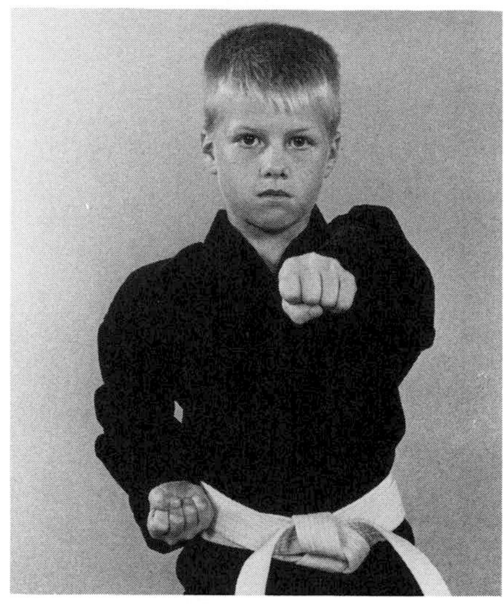

To punch again, push the right hand out while pulling the left hand back quickly.

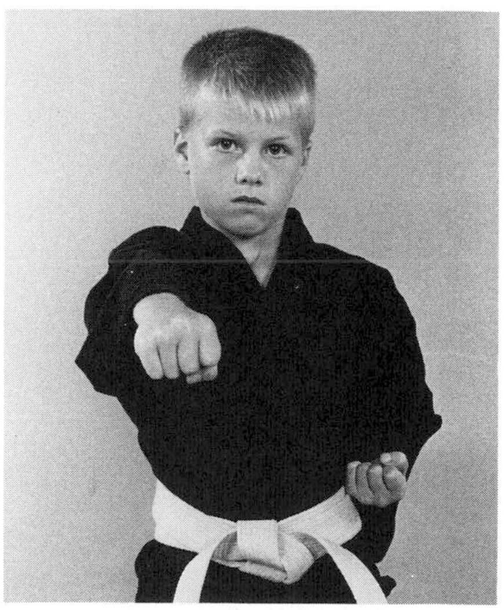

Punch again with the left hand. Just remember that when you punch, the positions of the hands are reversed.

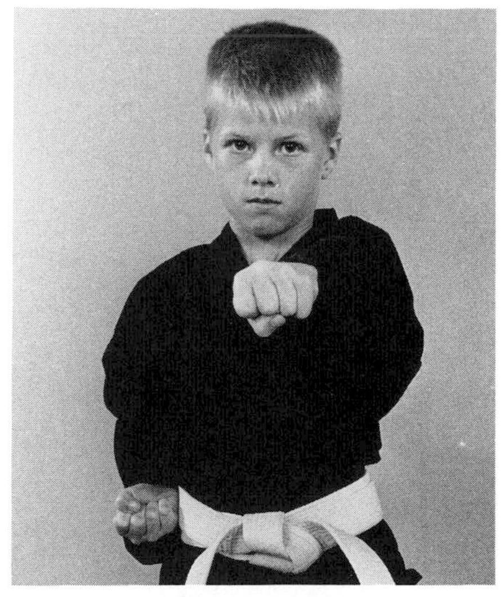

With practice, you will be able to make a fist and punch easily without following each step and stopping to think about it.

The Stances

The karate stance is the most important part of karate. Everything is built upon the stance. To do a good kick, you must have a good stance. To do a good block, you must have a good stance. The three basic stances are the front stance, . . .

. . . the back stance, and . . .

. . . the horse stance.

1

2

3

To move into a front stance: Stand in what is called an open stance, with your feet placed apart as widely as your shoulders **(1)**.

Next, move your left foot in close to your right foot **(2)**. Keep your left heel off the floor.

Then move your left foot forward in front of you **(3)**. Begin to bend your left knee and keep your right knee straight. Both feet are pointed straight ahead.

Move completely into the left front stance by pushing your left leg out fully. Over one-half of your weight is on your left leg. It is deeply bent, while the right leg is kept straight. To do a right front stance, move your right foot in front and place the left leg behind, reversing the process.

A little more difficult to do is the back stance. To get into a right back stance, start in an open stance.

Move to the right by putting your right foot out to your side. Your right foot is facing to your right and your left foot is straight in front of you.

To move into the stance, pull your right foot straight behind you and place a little over one-half of your weight on the right leg. Bend the front leg slightly and lower your body into the stance. Reverse the steps to do a left back stance. In a left back stance, your left leg is placed behind you and the right leg is in front.

To get into a horse stance, start in an open stance.

Simply lift your left foot and slide it out to your left.

Move your left foot out to two times the width of your shoulders, and bend both of your knees deeply.

Blocks

You are now ready to do three of the major blocks, known as the lower block, . . .

. . . the center block, and . . .

. . . the upper block.

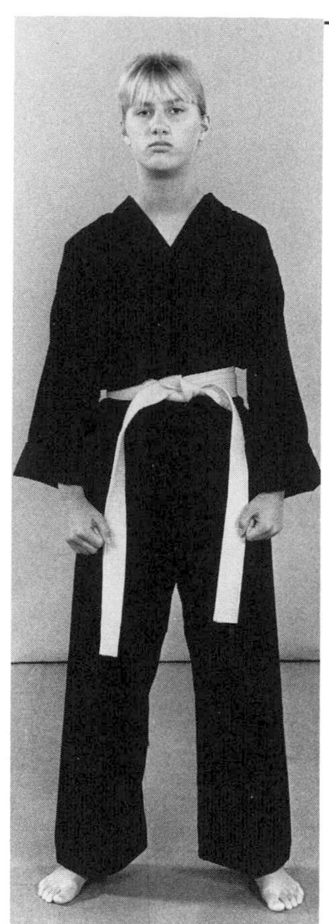

To do a lower block, stand in the ready stance.

Next, pull your left hand, closed into a fist, across your face near your right ear.

Push your left hand downwards, while you also lower your right hand.

As you continue to bring down your left arm to block, begin pulling your right arm back tightly to your side.

Snap the left arm down into a block and pull your right arm tight by your side with your fist in an upside down position, ready to punch if needed.

To do the center block, get into the open stance.

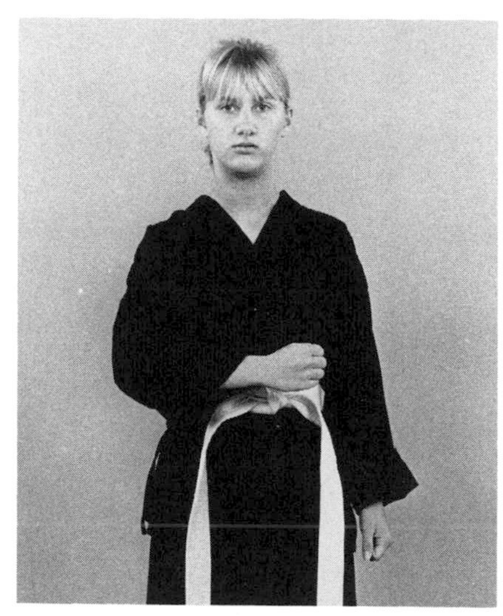

Bring your right arm in front of you at belt level. The palm of your hand is facing you, but the fist is closed.

Snap your right arm straight up and pull the left arm back to your left side at the same time. This will give your block more power. You can reverse the process to block with your left arm.

To do an upper block, get into a left back stance and place your left hand straight out in front of you. Your right hand is at your right side, ready to begin the block.

Bring your right arm across your body in front of your neck. Begin to pull your left arm in towards your side.

Snap the right arm upwards and jerk the left arm back at the same time. To do a left-arm upper block, reverse your arms and do the same steps.

Strikes

In addition to the front punch, there are other basic strikes. These include the backfist, back elbow strike, and the knifehand, or "karate chop."

To throw a backfist strike, pull your arm close to your chest with your palm facing your chest.

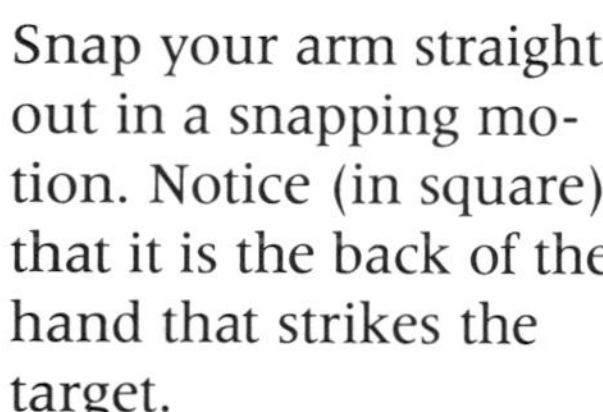

Snap your arm straight out in a snapping motion. Notice (in square) that it is the back of the hand that strikes the target.

Just as fast as you struck out with the backfist, snap your arm back to your chest. This is like the snapping of a whip: It will give your strike more power.

To do the back elbow strike, push your right arm straight out in front of you.

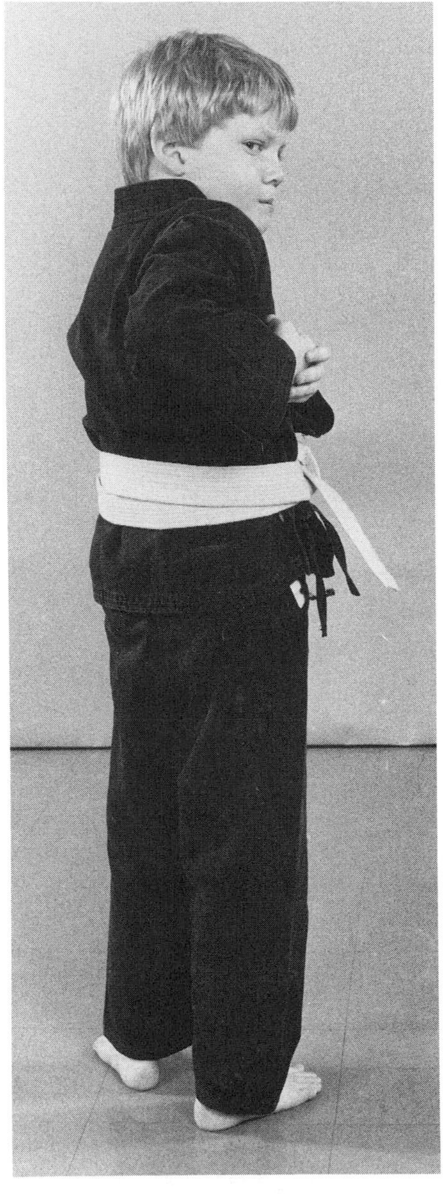

Place your left hand over your right hand and push your right arm back hard, striking with the elbow.

To strike with the knifehand, pull your right arm up so your hand is behind your right ear. Push your left hand slightly forward.

Turn your open hand and begin bringing it around.

With a snapping movement, strike the target with the bottom edge of your hand as you pull your left arm tight to your waist at the same time.

Kicks

Now you are ready to learn the three basic kicks. These are the front kick, the side kick, and the roundhouse kick.

From a left front stance, you can do a right front kick.

Bring your right knee up and keep your heel close to your hips.

Pull your toes back as you begin to push the foot outward.

Snap the leg out into a front kick. Notice that you strike with the ball of your foot, the part you land on when you jump up and down on your toes. To do a left front kick, get into a right front stance and follow the same steps.

To throw a side kick, get into an open stance.

Pull your right foot in towards the left knee.

Begin to snap the leg out . . .

. . . and fully lock your leg by snapping it completely out. You strike the opponent with the outside edge of the foot. You can do the same kick with the left leg, while standing on the right.

To do a roundhouse kick, stand in either a front or back stance.

Bring your right leg up, keeping your foot behind you as far as possible.

Begin to push the leg out and around . . .

. . . until it is fully extended. You strike the opponent with the ball of the foot. You can do the roundhouse kick with the left leg by changing to your other side.

You now have been introduced to the basic tools of karate and are ready to put these blocks, kicks, and punches together for some real karate action.

Putting It All Together

Now let's put all of the karate skills that you have learned together in useful patterns.

Patterns

Pattern 1
Get into a left front stance with your left arm in a lower left block.

Leaving your arms in the same position, pull your right foot up next to your left foot. Place some of your weight on the ball of your right foot for balance.

Then step up into a right front stance and do a right punch at the same time. Remember, to give power to your punch, jerk the left hand back at the same time you strike out with the punch. Keep your left hand upside down by your side.

With your right hand also in the same position, pull your left leg up just as before.

Do a left karate punch as you move into a left front stance.

From an open stance, . . . move into a left front stance and prepare to block with a left center block.

Complete the left center block.

Cross your arms and prepare to do a right center block.

Complete the right center block.

Pattern 3
In a horse stance, do a left upper block.

Punch to the center area with a right front punch.

Punch to the head area with a left front punch.

Punch to the lower area with a right front punch.

Pattern 4
Do a right front kick as you do an upper block with your left hand.

Place the leg and foot back into a left front stance and do a right front punch to the head.

Finish with a left punch to the head area.

Pattern 5
Do a left upper block . . .

. . . and deliver a front kick.

Return to the front stance and punch with the right hand to the head area.

Pattern 6
Do a left lower block as you move into a left front stance.

Do a front snap kick to the head area and then . . .

. . . step back into the stance and throw a left front punch to the head area.

Pattern 7
Do a center block while in a left front stance.

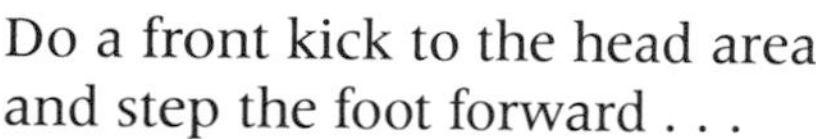
Do a front kick to the head area and step the foot forward . . .

. . . into a right front stance as you do a right front punch.

Pattern 8
Move into a right back stance as you do a left center block.

Drop the hand down into a lower left block.

While still in the back stance, do a right roundhouse kick.

Pattern 9
In a right back stance, block with a left center block.

Then do a knifehand strike to the neck area . . .

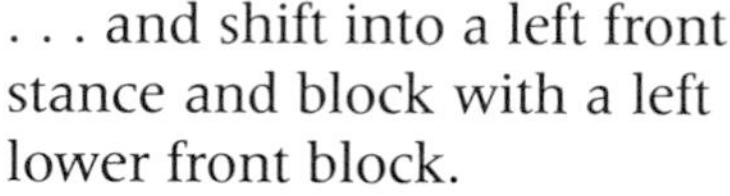

. . . and shift into a left front stance and block with a left lower front block.

Step up into a right front stance and do a right front punch to the head area.

Pattern 10
From an open stance . . .

. . . move into a left front stance with a left center block.

Next, shift back into a right back stance and do a right front punch.

Quickly, do a right front kick and . . .

. . . step down into a right front stance.

Finish with a left side kick to the chest.

Now you are ready to practise with a partner. Be careful and **do not hit** your partner. Stop your punches or kicks one to two inches from the target.

Partner Combinations

Practise these sparring moves very slowly until they come easily and you have good control of your strikes. Make up your own moves. Remember, do not actually hit and always be careful.

Sequence 1
Have your partner stand in a left front stance with his hand raised to strike downward, like a hammer. You stand in an open stance with your hands at your sides.

Block the blow with a left upper block as you move into a left front stance.

Then step forward and deliver a knifehand to the neck.

Finish with a low left front punch to the stomach.

Sequence 2

Face your partner as he prepares to punch.

Move back into a right back stance as you block a center punch with a left center block.

Finish with a right roundhouse kick to your partner's head.

Sequence 3
Block your partner's left center punch with a right center block as you remain in an open stance.

Do a quick front kick with your left leg to the chest area.

Sequence 4
Prepare to block another punch.

This time do a right front kick to the stomach area.

Then from the kick step forward into a right front stance and do a right front punch at the same time.

Sequence 5
Block your partner's right center punch with a left center block.

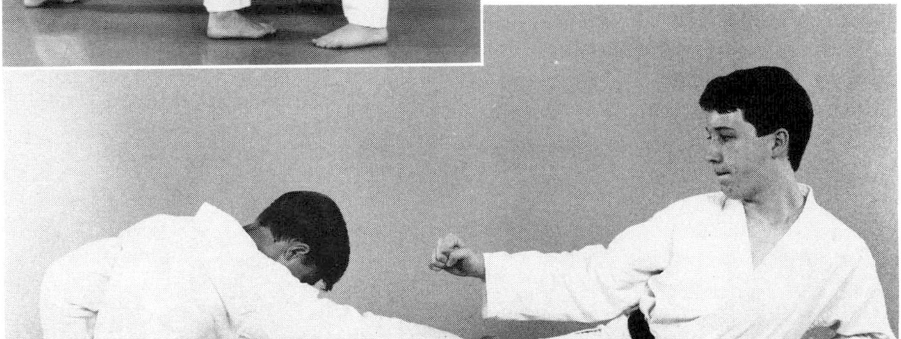

Finish with a right side kick to the lower stomach area.

Sequence 6
Block a lower kick with a lower left block.

Throw a fast roundhouse kick to the head.

Sequence 7
Step up and punch with a right punch to the head.

Step up again with the left leg and do a left front punch to the head.

As you practise these combinations, you will get faster and faster. You will also learn to make up your own. You can see that karate is like putting a puzzle together. One karate technique fits into another and you just keep building. Now it is time to learn a little about the sport of karate.

Sports Karate

In sports karate you will learn how to compete for trophies and awards.

Tournaments

On weekends, karate tournaments are held all over the world. Look in popular karate magazines for places and times.

You will see boys and girls of all ages at tournaments.

When you register, you are given a number for each event you enter.

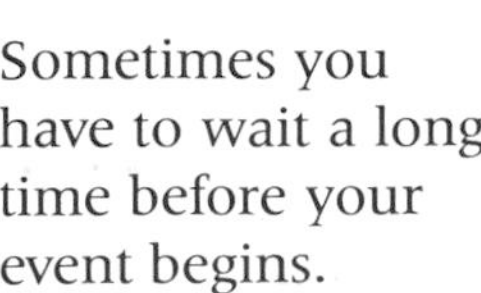

Sometimes you have to wait a long time before your event begins.

You can enter two major events. One event is called kata *(ka-tuh)* and is the karate dance. There are many katas, from very simple to very difficult.

The other event is called kumite *(koo-mah-tay)*. Kumite is sparring. You will spar with opponents the same age, size, and rank as you are.

In karate, you are in either the beginner division (white, yellow, and orange belts), the intermediate division (green and blue belts), the advanced division (brown belt), or the expert division (black belt).

When you compete in kata, you face the judges, usually three, and with their permission begin your kata.

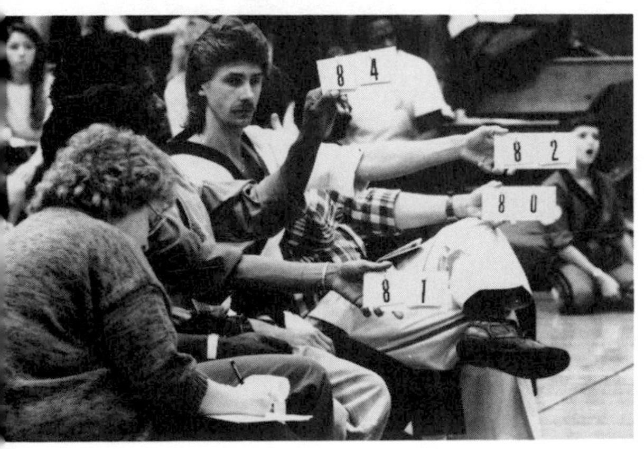

Katas are judged on a scale from 1.0 to 10. Some common scores for beginners are 3.4 or 4.6. The scores are averaged and the highest four scores win first, second, third, and fourth places.

Kata

Now you are going to learn a kata. Kata will help you improve your ability, even if you never enter a tournament. This kata is called Sheno II.

Stand in a closed stance, with your feet together.

Bow.

Move into a left front stance and do a lower left block.

Still in the left front stance, follow with a center right front punch . . .

. . . then a left upper punch to the face.

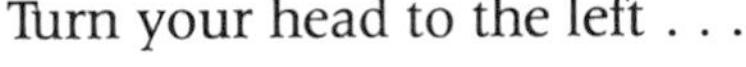

Turn your head to the left . . .

. . . and move your left foot back and pointing to the left.

Turn and move into a left upper block in a left front stance.

Next, do a right front kick to chest level.

Bring your foot back into the original stance and punch with a right upper front punch.

Follow with a left upper front punch to the head area.

Slide your right foot back, moving into a horse stance with both of your hands in punching position.

Do a right front kick.

Bring your kick back and do a right front punch to the head area.

Next, punch with the left hand.

Turn your head to the right and do a lower right block to your right side.

Prepare to do a backfist strike.

Complete the strike.

Turn your body to the right and do a right lower block in a right front stance.

Do a front kick to the stomach area.

Bring your foot back to a right front stance and do a left front punch to the head.

Follow up with a right punch to head level.

Bring your left foot back and stand in an open stance.

End the kata by bringing your feet together in a closed stance.

Bow.

Kumite

You will also have the opportunity to compete in kumite. Each match is two minutes long. During the match, the first person to score three points wins. If nobody scores a total of three points, the person with the most points at the end wins the match.

There are three to five judges for each match.

To score a point, you must get a punch within two inches (5 cm) of a target area (head, chest, or stomach) without the punch or kick being blocked.

After a strike, the judges vote to award or not to award a point.

Two of the three judges must agree that a point was scored.

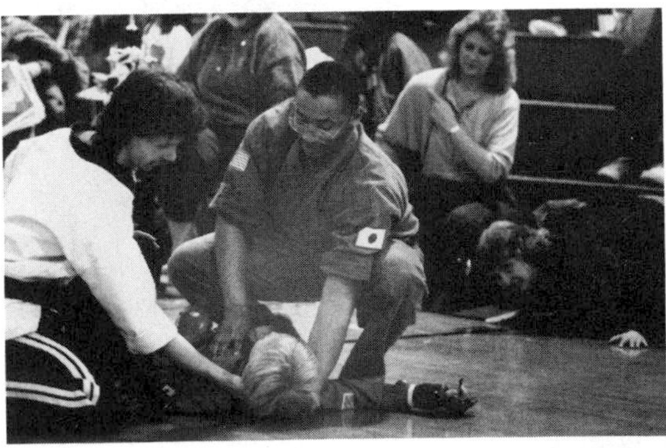

Sometimes the sparring action can become too furious and you can get hurt. You will be reminded to be careful.

Now you can practise with a partner and try these kumite techniques.

If your partner throws a low kick, block it with a lower block . . .

. . . and do a quick side kick to the chest.

If your partner throws a punch to your head, block it with an upper block, then . . .

. . . throw a fast front kick to your opponent's stomach for the point.

If your opponent throws a center punch to your body, block it with a center block, then . . .

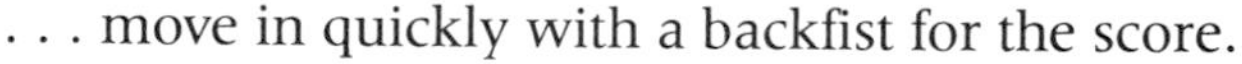

. . . move in quickly with a backfist for the score.

Block a roundhouse kick with a center block and . . .

. . . strike with a roundhouse kick to the head for the point.

Block your opponent's punch to the head with an upper block.

Strike back with a right front kick to the stomach. If it is blocked, . . .

. . . spin the foot around into a roundhouse kick to the head for the score.

Sparring or kumite can be fun in a tournament, at karate class, or in your garage. Just remember to be careful.

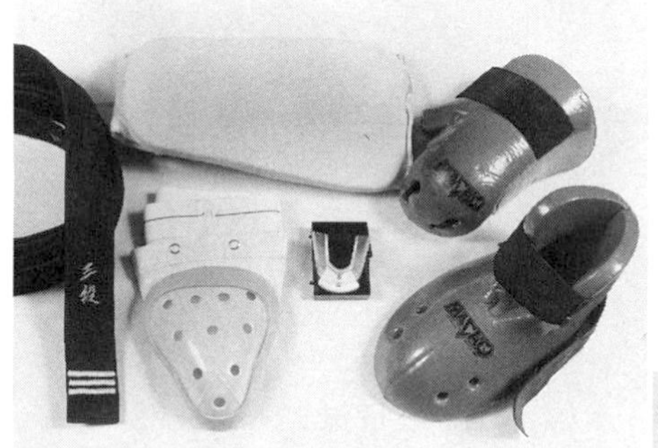

If you spar, or kumite, you will need some equipment. Gloves, protective supporters for boys, shin guards, and mouth guards (shown here) are designed to protect you.

To be really safe, use hand and foot gloves and protective head gear.

Remember to be a good sport, win or lose.

Learning Karate

You can learn basic karate from this book. However, to learn more, find a caring, well qualified instructor.

There are many instructors who work well with children. Get your parents to help you find a good instructor. Look in the telephone book or check with your local Y for classes. Ask to visit a class to observe before joining.

Many good instructors charge reasonable rates (about $40 to $60 per month). Avoid contracts or large fees. Make sure the instructor is at least a first-degree black belt.

Remember that discipline is important and you will enjoy being part of a group. Have respect for your instructor because he or she worked hard to earn the black belt. It usually takes between four and eight years to earn one. Be wary of promises that you can earn a black belt in less than that time.

If you join a karate school, listen to your instructor and follow his or her direction and guidance.

When practising by yourself or in class, have patience, . . .

. . . work hard, . . .

. . . then harder, . . .

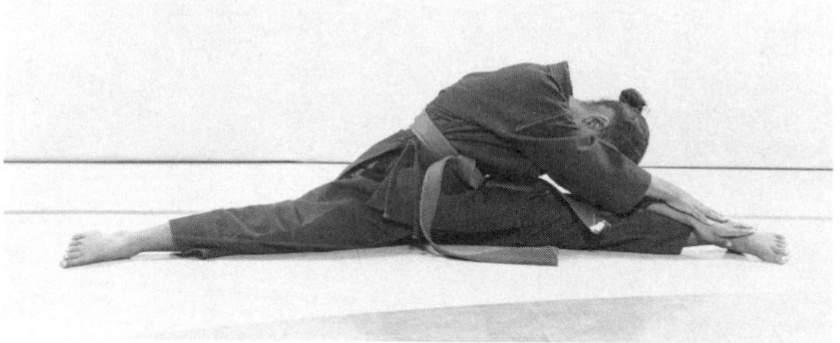

. . . and then even harder, . . .

. . . until you master every karate skill.

Always wear your mouth-piece when you spar . . .

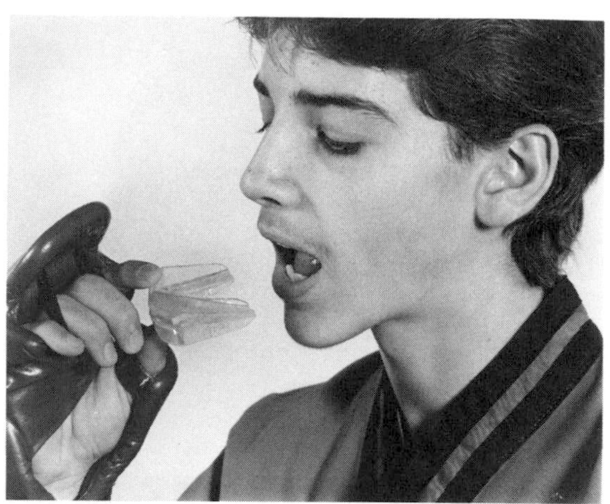

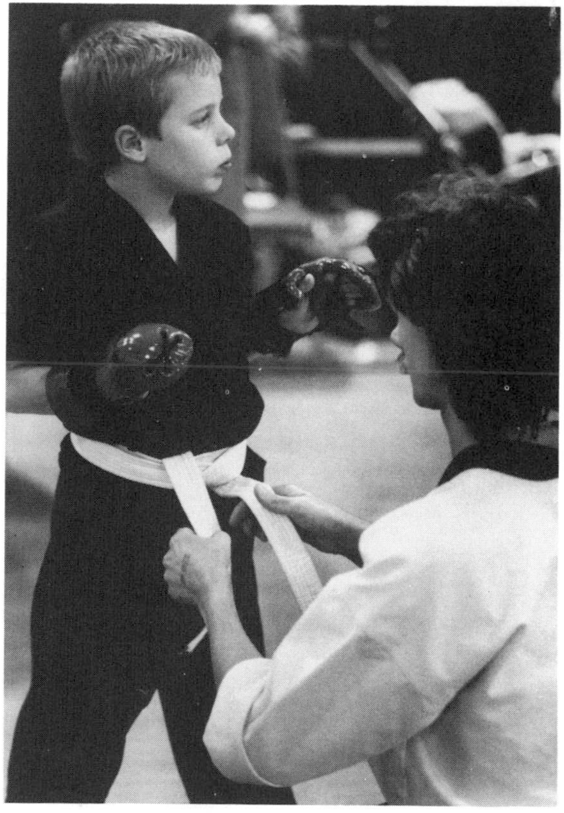

. . . and make sure you tie your belt.

Good luck in your study of karate. May you grow wiser as the years pass and may good health be your constant companion.

Index